Turning the World Upside Down

The Kingdom of God in Matthew's Gospel

An inductive Bible Study for individuals and groups

by Mike Jelliffe

NENGE BOOKS, Australia

Turning the World Upside Down: The Kingdom of God in Matthew's Gospel

by Mike Jelliffe

Published by NENGE BOOKS, Australia, April 2019

ABN 26809396184

Email: nengebooks1@gmail.com

www.nengebooks.com

Copyright © 2019 Michael A Jelliffe

All rights reserved.

This book or parts thereof may not be reproduced in any form, stored in a retrieval system, or transmitted in any form - electronic, mechanical, photocopy, recoirding or otherwise - without prior permission of the publisher.

First revision, June 2019

Book layout & cover design by NENGE BOOKS

Cover photos © 2019 Michael A Jelliffe.

References taken from *Jesus Through Middle Eastern Eyes* by Kenneth E. Bailey, Copyright © 2008 by Kenneth E. Bailey, used by permission of Intervarsity Press, PO Box 1400, Downers Grover, IL 60515, USA.

This book available at wholesale bulk rates for churches. Leader's Guide also available. Email nengebooks1@gmail to order.

ISBN 978-0-6484284-3-5

> *"These who turned the Roman empire upside down.... saying there is another king of a different nature, Jesus."*
>
> Acts 17:6-7 (Wuest 1984)

A consistent theme that Matthew records in his gospel is that of the Kingdom of God, also referred to as the kingdom of heaven by Matthew, in respect of his Jewish readers who did not directly use the name of God.

This inductive Bible study centered in the gospel of Matthew looks at how the Kingdom of God formed the backbone of Jesus' teaching and ministry, and how it applies to the church today.

A Leader's Guide is available from the publisher and recommended for group leaders and trainers using this study book.

📖 Indicates a Bible passage to read. Then answer the question following. For groups, discuss the question together before finalising your answer.

Contents

1. INTRODUCING JESUS	7
Matthew Introduces Jesus' Genealogy	7
Events at Jesus' Conception	10
2. EVENTS AT JESUS' BIRTH	14
Visit of the Wise Men from the East	14
3. JESUS' PREPARATION FOR MINISTRY	21
John the Baptist's Ministry	21
John in Prison	23
4. THE TEMPTATIONS OF JESUS	27
Bread	27
Temple	30
Mountaintop	32
5. THE COMMISSION OF JESUS	38
Sabbatical Year	39
Jubilee Year	40
Jesus commences His ministry	41
6. THE CHARACTER OF THE KINGDOM	47
Demonstrating the Kingdom	47
The Beatitudes	49
Turning the law upside-down	50
7. KINGDOM BEHAVIOUR	54
Giving to the poor	54
The Lord's Prayer	54
Fasting	56
Possessions and money	56
Food, drink and clothing, life's worries	56

8. JESUS & THE RELIGIOUS LEADERS	61
Sabbath Day Observance	61
Clean and Unclean	63
Breaking Rules of Piety	64
Cleansing the temple	65
9. THE FULFILLMENT OF THE KINGDOM	69
Entering the Kingdom of God	71
The Consummation of the Kingdom of God	75
10. KINGDOM AND JUDGEMENT	81
The Parable of the Tenants	81
The Parable of the Weeds	82
The Parable of the Net	83
The Final Judgement	84
The Parable of the Talents	85
The Parable of the Sheep and Goats	85
Parable of the Unmerciful Servant	86
The Parable of the Ten Unmarried Women	87
11. KINGDOM AND CHURCH	90
Bibliography	100

Turning the World

STUDY 1

INTRODUCING JESUS
Matthew 1

Matthew Introduces Jesus' Genealogy.

 Read Matthew 1:1-17

Vs 1: Which two ancestors does Matthew trace Jesus to in this verse?

David, Abraham

Considering his readers were mainly Jewish, why do you think it was important for him to link Jesus to these two people?

Vs 6: What title does Matthew acknowledge, especially when he calls Jesus the "son of" this person in vs 1?

 Read Isaiah 9:6-7

This prophesy about the birth of the Messiah, the coming ruler, would have been familiar to Matthew's Jewish readers.

How is the Messiah linked to David?

Turning the World

List the names and attributes of this child ruler:

What message do you think Matthew is telling his readers by starting his gospel historically introducing Jesus this way?

Matthew lists five women in the genealogy of Jesus. Who are these women and what do you know about them? Are they Jews or Gentiles? Are they saints or sinners?

Tamar – Genesis 38;

Rahab – Joshua 6:17;

Ruth – the book of Ruth;

Uriah's wife, Bathsheba - 2 Samuel 11;

Mary, mother of Jesus.

Upside Down

Why do you think Matthew included them in the history of Jesus and what is Matthew telling us about the future ministry of Jesus?

 Matthew 8:20; 11:19

Jesus used two expressions about who He was as "the Son of…". What does He call himself in these verses?

 Daniel 7:13-14

Daniel describes seeing this person in a vision. As you read these verses, how would you describe in a word what this person is (what is his authority and role)?

 Matthew 24:30

How do these verses describe who this person is and what He is doing?

How do these verses relate to the verses in Daniel?

So Matthew establishes who Jesus is both by grounding him as a son of man though His genealogy, but also identifying Him as the Son of Man, the coming King, fulfilling OT prophesy.

Turning the World

📖 Matthew 3:16-17

Whose voice calls from heaven after His baptism, and what does He call Jesus?

📖 Matthew 4:3, 6

This is the second "son of " title given to Jesus. In this verse it is used by Satan, Jesus' tempter in the desert.

He challenges that Jesus is the Son of Who?

Satan is directly challenging God's spoken word. How does Jesus respond to Satan?

This title for Jesus clearly relates to His divinity.

Events at Jesus' Conception

If Jesus is the Son of Man and the Son of God, we would expect to see some evidence of this from his birth. What events in the following verses in Matthew 1 highlight that Jesus was indeed from God and a King?

📖 Matthew 1:18

How was Jesus conceived?

Upside Down

 1:19

What was different about how Joseph treated Mary? Is this what most men would do if they found their fiancée was pregnant before they were married? Why did he treat her this way?

 1:20

How does God speak to Joseph?

 1:21

How was Jesus conceived and who decided his name?

 1:22-23

What other name would he have, and what does this name tell us about him?

 1:24

How does Joseph respond to what the angel tells him?

Turning the World

REFLECTION

What new understanding of Jesus and His ministry have you learnt through this study so far?

While Mary the mother of Jesus is highlighted in Luke's gospel story, Matthew highlights the character of Joseph. What qualities do you think God saw in Joseph to be the earthly step-father of Jesus?

What character qualities would God find in you if He needed you for an important role like this? Why do you think He would chose you or not?

Notes

STUDY 2

EVENTS AT JESUS' BIRTH
Matthew 2

We would also expect to see evidence from those who observed Jesus after his birth that He was the "Son of Man", the Messiah.

Visit of the Wise Men from the East

 Matthew 2:1-12

These rich scholars were no doubt leaders in their own communities in what is now the Middle Eastern countries of Jordon and Saudi Arabia, west of Palestine. They were Arabs (Gentiles) who understood astrology, mathematics and science of the day, as well as the Jewish Scriptures and prophesies. Kenneth Bailey[1] notes that in 1920 a Bedouin tribe was discovered in Jordon whose tribal name meant "those who study/follow the planets". They claimed that they had ancestors who had journeyed to Palestine to see the prophet Jesus.

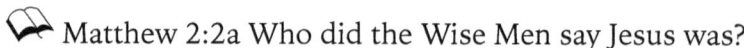 Matthew 2:2a Who did the Wise Men say Jesus was?

2:2b What was the sign they identified?

Numbers 24:17-19 If they were thinking of it as fulfilling this prophesy, what kind of person were they looking for?

---

1. Taken from *Jesus Through Middle Eastern Eyes* by Kenneth E. Bailey. Copyright © 2008 by Kenneth E. Bailey. Used by permission of Intervarsity Press, PO Box 1400, Downers Grover, IL 60515, USA. p.53

Upside Down

What will happen to Israel as a result of this person?

What will happen to all the other nations mentioned (Edom/Seir, Moab and Sheth, non-Jewish peoples to the east of Israel)?

Why do you think these wise men came (from these nations to the east) to worship Jesus, what may have been their motive?

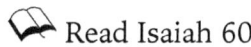 Read Isaiah 60.

In Isaiah's mind, this is a prophesy about Jerusalem (see vs 14).

vs 6 specifically mentions what events similar to those in Matthew 2:1-12?

While Isaiah was speaking about Jerusalem, this prophesy did not happen for Jerusalem.

In how many ways is this prophesy fulfilled by Jesus?

Turning the World

How does this prophesy now shift the focus from the nation of Israel to Jesus as the King of all the nations?

The gates of Jerusalem were always shut for security, so vs 11 must have a future fulfillment. From vs 17-21, list the things which will be the marks of this new Kingdom of God:

📖 Matthew 2:3 Why do you think Herod was disturbed by the news from the wise men?

📖 2:4-5 Who does Herod identify this ruler as?

📖 Read also John 7:41-42.

'Christ' is the Greek word for the Hebrew word 'Messiah'. King Herod was a Jew religiously and knew that the Scriptures promised the coming of the Messiah as a conquering King.

Upside Down

 Read Micah 5:2-4

This is the OT prophesy that Herod's chief priests and advisors correctly identified as telling the birth place of Jesus in Bethlehem.

From Micah's prophesy, Matthew 2:6 says that from Bethlehem will come a person who has two roles. What are they?

1.

2.

 Matthew 2:8

Herod also searched for Jesus but for a different reason. Did he really want to also worship Jesus? What do you think was his true motive and why was he troubled by Jesus' birth?

From this story, do you think the wise men had any doubts about Jesus being a King?

Do you think Herod had any doubts about Jesus being a King?

 2:11 The wise men present their gifts to the baby Jesus. What were the three gifts?

The significance of the wise men's actions helps us see how absolutely confident the men were that this newborn baby was to be the King over all nations.

"Gold is a precious metal and as such was a very valuable commodity. Its value could very well have financed Joseph and Mary's trip to Egypt. The Bible does not tell us any other significance to these three gifts; however, tradition has it that there is a deeper meaning for each of the three. Gold is a symbol of divinity and is mentioned throughout the Bible. Pagan idols were often made from gold and the Ark of the Covenant was overlaid with gold (Exodus 25:10-17). The gift of gold to the Christ child was symbolic of His divinity—God in flesh.

"Frankincense is a white resin or gum. It is obtained from a tree by making incisions in the bark and allowing the gum to flow out. It is highly fragrant when burned and was therefore used in worship, where it was burned as a pleasant offering to God (Exodus 30:34). Frankincense is a symbol of holiness and righteousness. The gift of frankincense to the Christ child was symbolic of His willingness to become a sacrifice, wholly giving Himself up, analogous to a burnt offering.

"Myrrh was also a product of Arabia, and was obtained from a tree in the same manner as frankincense. It was a spice and was used in embalming. It was also sometimes mingled with wine to form an article of drink. Such a drink was given to our Saviour when He was about to be crucified, as a stupefying potion (Mark 15:23). Matthew 27:34 refers to it as "gall." Myrrh symbolizes bitterness, suffering, and affliction. The baby Jesus would grow to suffer greatly as a man and would pay the ultimate price when He gave His life on the cross for all who would believe in Him.[2]

---

2. From "Why did the Magi bring gold, frankincense, and myrrh to Jesus?", internet article in www.gotquestions.org.

Upside Down

Summary

Matthew introduces Jesus as totally Jewish historically yet also affirms His divine Messianic Kingship in the events of His birth. From Daniel to David, Herod to the Magi, there is recognition of Jesus' authority over Jew and Gentile, saint and sinner.

REFLECTION

When you consider the response to Jesus by the wise men and by King Herod, you see very different attitudes to Jesus and very different ways in which they approached Jesus. Yet both acknowledged Him as Messiah and King.

What were their motives in wishing to see the baby Jesus and how did their actions achieve their individual motives?

How do people in your community acknowledge Jesus? Do they recognise Him as King or is this a foreign concept?

How do different people's attitudes to Jesus affect the way they approach Him?

What motives do people have for believing in Jesus today?

What is your motive for following Jesus?

Turning the World

Notes

STUDY 3

JESUS' PREPARATION FOR MINISTRY
Matthew 3

John the Baptist's Ministry

 Read Matthew 3:1-17

3:2, 8 What was John's main message?

3:3 What did John see as his own ministry and role? Who was he preparing the way for?

 Read Luke 3:4-6

Luke records the whole prophesy from Isaiah which refers to John. What are five things that are going to change when the Lord comes?

1. vs5

2.

3.

4.

Turning the World

5. vs 6

📖 **Matthew 3:11, 14** How did John rate himself against the one who was to come, even when he identified him as his cousin?

📖 **Matthew 3:12**

John gives a picture of what the One to come would do, using picture language which would be familiar to his listeners, village people who were used to harvesting wheat. When he talks about this person having a harvesting fork in his hand, clearing the threshing floor, gathering the wheat into his storehouse, and burning the chaff (rubbish left over after separating the wheat grain from the plant), how would you describe this person's role in everyday language?

What additional element does this role add to that of Messiah and King already discussed earlier?

We have already noted that the baptism of Jesus is marked by the opening of heaven, the Spirit of God descending on Him, and the voice from heaven clearly announcing the Sonship of Jesus, all clearly pointing to His divinity as the Son of God.

Upside Down

After preaching that the Kingdom of Heaven is near, and then anointing Jesus as the one who will be the central person in that kingdom, what message do you think John continued to preach?

John in Prison

 Matthew 11:1-19

Jesus has travelled to Galilee and word of His ministry reaches John who is in prison. Despite John's confidence that Jesus was the One, and conducting His baptism, John seems to have some other thoughts now. Herod Antipas, a son of Herod the Great who tried to kill Jesus as a baby, was now ruling Galilee.

 Matthew 14:3-5

Why did Herod put John in prison?

Do you think John was still preaching his main message?

 Matthew 11:3

Why do you think John now asks this question about Jesus?

 vs 4-6 What does Jesus tell the disciples to say to John?

Turning the World

Would you consider these things as normal for a man to do, or do they indicate another power, or kingdom, at work?

Jesus' reply is this, tell John about what you are seeing and hearing – that the miracles and things that are happening are things which demonstrate the Kingdom of God. Therefore you can be sure about who I am.

 Acts 19:1-7

How successful was John in preparing people for the coming of Jesus? How far had John's disciples spread?

Summary

John announces that the kingdom of heaven is near, turning people to repentance, baptising them and telling them of the Messiah who was to come. But once in prison, he had his doubts.

REFLECTION

How does hardship sometimes affect how we see the things we used to be sure about?

Are there things which you were sure about in your faith that you now doubt? What are they?

How does Jesus' reply to John help you to understand that the Kingdom of God is a reality even if we don't see it at times?

Notes

STUDY 4

THE TEMPTATIONS OF JESUS
Matthew 4

 Read Matthew 4:1-11

In the three temptations of Jesus, Satan tries to rob Jesus of His God given authority as Messiah. The temptations challenge Jesus' kingship over three major aspects of society.

Temptation 1 - Bread

In vs 1-3 what potential weakness in Jesus does Satan target in this first temptation?

Vs 4 What does Jesus say to respond and why does this response satisfy Satan?

In Jesus' day, the population of Galilee was about 350,000 people, most living in poverty, with many having little or no education, "ignorant of the fine points of the law", and "overwhelmed with the burden of making a living" [3]. Small peasant farmers were being pushed off their land by ruthless creditors. The Roman political leaders and Jewish religious leaders, Pharisees and Saducees, were amassing land holdings, and people were suffering under a system of double taxes extracted by both Jewish religious and

---
3. Kraybill 1978 p.84

Turning the World

Roman civil civil tax systems.

> ".... most scholars agree that between forty and seventy percent of the peasants annual income eventually fell into the hands of various kinds of creditors and tax collectors" (Kraybill p.86).

A very definite two tiered society had emerged, the rich and the struggling poor, which was the vast majority of people, who were squashed down by the structures of society designed to make the rich get richer.

"Bread symbolises the heart of economic life" in many societies, just like rice, kaukau, sago or yams do in Asian and Melanesian societies. "It stands for the basic necessities of life."[4]

When Jesus instructed the disciples to pray, 'Give us today our daily bread' (Matthew 6:11) immediately after praying for His Kingdom to come, we see a deeper meaning evident.

 Read Matthew 14:13-21

Vs 14 What was Jesus' heart response to the crowds who were hungry and sick?

Vs 17-21 What was his practical response to their hunger?

 Read John 6:26-40

Vs 26 Why do you think the crowds followed Jesus?

Do you think Jesus was aware of the power he had to draw in crowds by feeding them and so become a 'welfare' King?

---

4. Kraybill 1978 p.80

Upside Down

Vs 27-29 What does Jesus say is the right attitude?

The bread motif in Jesus' teaching is a major one. In this temptation Satan also tries to devalue the deeper meaning of bread as the sustainer of life.

Vs 35 What does Jesus say is the true bread of life?

 Read Luke 22:19

What does Jesus say is the new bread?

 Read Luke 24:30-31

When did the two disciples going to Emmaus recognise Jesus?

The temptation of Jesus to turn stones into bread was much more than just fulfilling his hunger, severe as that was at the time. Kraybill[5] comments:

> This bread temptation in the wilderness focused squarely on the economic structures of Palestine that created and perpetuated hungry masses...
>
> When the values of Jesus' Kingdom become the bread of life, the economic institutions of society lose their grip on their human slaves. Rich persons suddenly realise there is new eternal bread. In that realisation they begin sharing liberally so that there is even mundane bread for all. .... Rich persons moved by God's mercy and filled with joyous liberation from their economic taskmasters, stop hoarding and give liberally...
>
> His life and teaching brought a straightforward condemnation on the institutional structures that trample over poor people to make rich people richer.

5. Kraybill 1978 p.81, 92-93

Turning the World

Other stories in Matthew's gospel where Jesus challenges the rich or the economic structures of society which had become corrupt to favour the rich:

Read Matthew 22:15-22; Matthew 19:16-30; Matthew 6:19-24

How would you summarise the main point of these stories?

Do you know any other stories in the gospels with a similar challenge?

Read Acts 4:32-37

How did the early church demonstrate these new Kingdom values?

How much do the economic structures of your society reflect these Kingdom of God values, and how much do they reflect the old values?

Temptation 2 - Temple

Read Matthew 4:5-6

What does Satan actually ask Jesus to do?

Vs 7 Why does this reply answer the temptation?

Upside Down

If the first temptation targeted Jesus' kingdom ministry at the economic level of structures in society and human need, what structure of society does this second temptation target?

If Jesus was to be accepted by the Jewish religious community as Messiah, what better entrance than to jump off the top of the Jerusalem Temple and be carried down into the midst of the priests and leaders in the arms of angels? But this temptation to be powerful in the religious structures of the day was not what God's Kingdom is all about. Once again Satan tempts Jesus to take a different path than the Kingdom of God. While he preached in synagogues and demonstrated total support for the Jewish religious system as expressed in the written Scriptures,

> he directly confronted institutionalised religion wherever and whenever it became idolatrous or oppressive in burdening the faithful... he replaced the machinery of formalised religion with compassion and love.[6]

 Read Matthew 8:1-4

How does Jesus show compassion and love by inclusion of an outcast who was unclean by Jewish law, while supporting the Jewish law for him to see the priest and make an offering (ref. Leviticus 14:1-32)?

 Read Matthew 12:1-14

What does Jesus say is of greatest value - people or the laws?

---

6. Kraybill 1978 p.77

Turning the World

vs8 Who is Lord of the Sabbath? What did Jesus mean by this statement?

 Read Matthew 23:13-31

What seven accusations (woes) does Jesus make of the Pharisees who loved legalism based on oral laws - laws not written but passed on by oral tradition to expand the written laws?

1. vs 13-14

2. vs 15-16

3. vs 16-22

4. vs 23-24

5. vs 25-26

6. vs 27-28

7. vs 29-32

Temptation 3 - Mountaintop

 Read Matthew 4:8-9

What institution does Satan target in this third temptation?

Upside Down

In the decades leading up to the time of Jesus, and indeed for nearly 70 years after his birth, there was guerrilla-type warfare led by Jewish Zealot nationalists trying to dislodge the Roman military occupation of Palestine. The Romans ruled by force, and activity against them was by force. The Jews were a people living in their own land but oppressed under Roman miltary rule. There was great expectation that the coming of the Messiah would be as a conquering King who would rid Israel of the Romans and restore it to the Jews. Even the disciples still thought this.

 Read Acts 1:6

How much about the new Kingdom of God do you think the disciples really understood even after Jesus' resurrection?

Satan's temptation once again intended to lead Him in a different direction, a direction of political power and "a lure to endorse the accepted mode of governing by coercion and force" [7].

Who does Jesus say are the powerful in God's Kingdom in these verses:

 Matthew 18:1-4

 Matthew 19:21-24

 Matthew 7:21-23

 Matthew 15:21-28

 Matthew 22:1-13

 Matthew 23:11-12

---

7. Kraybill p.58

Turning the World

Jesus taught a different idea of power. Those who are powerful in the Kingdom of God are the children, the slaves, the humble, the outcasts, the sinners and the powerless.

📖 Matthew 4:10-11 How does Jesus respond to this so that Satan knew he had no more ammunition and left Jesus alone?

Do you think Jesus continued to face challenges of temptation from Satan during his life? Can you give an example?

Do you think Satan was aware of who Jesus was? Explain why you think that?

Do you think Satan was more powerful than Jesus at this point in time?

How did Jesus disarm Satan's power?

From His responses to Satan, what was Jesus' attitude towards God?

📖 Read Philippians 2:5-8

The Apostle Paul wrote about Jesus' attitude. How would you describe this attitude in one word?

Upside Down

Vs 8 Paul says that Jesus was obedient to God and that led to His death. How do you see Jesus' obedience to God demonstrated in His responses to Satan during the temptations?

Following His temptations, Matthew records that Jesus returned to Galilee after hearing that John had been put into prison.

 Matthew 4:12-13

Why do you think Jesus went back to the remoter areas of Galilee when he heard that John was put in prison?

 Matthew 4:17

What message did Jesus now preach?

Summary

Jesus overcame Satan's temptations which targetted his lordship over economic, religious and political spheres of society, appealing to His vulnerability after His desert experience. In doing so Jesus asserted His Kingship over these three major areas of life.

Turning the World

REFLECTION

Satan's temptations came to Jesus not only as personal temptations, but as a way to sidetrack Him from his mission and message. The Kingdom of God turns upside-down the economic, political and religious institutions of the day.

Do you think there are similarities between these three institutions (economic, political & religious) in Jesus' time and today?

Following Jesus' example, when we face temptations, how can we respond to disarm Satan?

Why is it important that we know the Bible?

Is being in a position of authority and being humble a contradiction, are they opposites?

How can we be humble yet maintain our authority in Christ?

Upside Down

Notes

Turning the World

STUDY 5

THE COMMISSION OF JESUS
Luke 4:14-30

Immediately after the temptations of Jesus, Luke in his gospel adds a significant story, that of Jesus in the synagogue at Nazareth, his hometown.

📖 Read Luke 4:14-21 (also Isaiah 61:1-2)

Vs 18 Who has annointed Jesus for this ministry?

vs 18-19 What are the five things that Jesus is commissioned to do?

1.

2.

3.

4.

5.

vs 21 What does Jesus then say about this Scripture section?

Upside Down

By reading these verses, which are an Old Testament Messianic prophesy, and applying them to Himself, Jesus announces that He is the Messiah (which means 'the Anointed One'), fulfilling the prophesy of Isaiah. But He also takes His listeners further back to another Scripture.

Sabbatical Year

To proclaim freedom is the same as proclaiming liberty. The Jews were familiar with the 'year of the Lord's favour' as a special year in the Jewish calendar.

The Lord instituted a Sabbath year for the Hebrews, every seventh year. What happened in that year to:

 Leviticus 25:2-7 - the land?

 Deuteronomy 15:12-18 - slaves?

vs 13-15 What attitude should they have when releasing slaves and why?

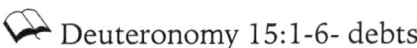 Deuteronomy 15:1-6- debts?

vs10-11 What attitude should they have towards the poor and why?

Turning the World

Jubilee Year

📖 Leviticus 25:8-54 - But a sabbatical of sabbatical years, the Jubilee year, added a further element of restoration.

vs 8 How often did the Jubilee year occur?

vs 9 How was the year announced?

vs 10 What is to be proclaimed throughout the land?

vs 13 Where is each person to go?

vs 11-12; 18-22 What can they eat?

vs 23 Who owns the land?

vs 14-16 How was land value to be determined?

How is this different from how land is valued commercially or in your community today?

How does Jubilee economics turn greed upside-down?

Upside Down

vs 17 What principle undermined transactions?

vs 24-34 What is redemption of the land or houses?

vs 35-38 What principle undermined how they should relate to the poor, and to outsiders (Gentiles)?

Jesus commences His ministry

Matthew resumes the story of Jesus as He commences His ministry in Galilee.

 Read Matthew 4:23-25

List all the works that Jesus did, and the kinds of people He ministered to.

How do these verses echo Luke 4:14-21?

Turning the World

 Read Matthew 11:2-6

How does Jesus answer John's question about whether He was the Messiah or not?

Jesus ministry was a reflection of Isaiah 61. It was a Jubilee ministry! Kraybill[8] notes

> Restoration is the prominent theme in the Jubilee and the common thread which ties together both the Nazarene sermon and Jesus' reply to John's disciples. Things will be restored back to their original state. There are images of paradise here. No more sweat. No more debts. No poverty. No more work. Slavery ends... Jubilee talk describes the Messiah's work. He announces that as of now God releases, lets go, and forgives our debts - our sins... The chains of sin are cut. Our eyes are opened. We are released from the captivity of evil. This is true liberation.

While Jubilee freedom points to a restoration of God's creation as it was in the garden of Eden, it also points to the coming of a new kingdom, the Kingdom of Heaven.

 Read Revelation 21:3-5

How do these verses in Revelation reflect the Jubilee message? What will people be free from?

---

8. Kraybill 1978 p.106-7

Upside Down

Returning to Luke 4, Bailey[9] suggests that by the use of specific format and words, Jesus edits the original Isaiah text when reading in the synagogue at Nazareth and clearly announces His messianic calling in three areas:

>   Proclamation (to preach good news to the poor)
>
>   Justice Advocacy (proclaim freedom for the prisoners)
>
>   Compassion (recovery of sight to the blind)
>
>   Justice Advocacy (release the oppressed)
>
>   Proclamation (proclaim the year of the Lord's favour)

Bailey[10] comments further:

> An act of compassion/love is placed in the centre of the list... A critical component of the challenge this text presents to the church in every age is to strive to keep this brilliant holistic package together. Each is meaningful, but only together in their christological setting do they achieve their full healing power.
>
> Every disciple of Jesus Christ has his or her special calling. The *preacher* knows that those marching for justice are an important part of the team. Thoughtful *justice advocates* know that the justice of God must judge the justice for which they strive. Those who show *compassion*, in whatever form, realise that without a message that changes hearts and without a just society, their work is incomplete. The greatest of all is love.

The home crowd in the synagogue at Nazareth initially seemed to accept Jesus and his words (vs 22) though Bailey[11] indicates translation of the original text is better understood as them being angry from the time Jesus finished reading the Isaiah passage, sat down and began speaking.

 Read Luke 4:23-27

In his additional comments, who are the two people (and what is their cultural status) who Jesus says received God's mercy and blessing through Elijah and Elisha, when people in Israel were suffering?

---

9. Bailey 2008 p.149ff.
10. Bailey 2008 p.161-162
11. Bailey 2008 p.151

Turning the World

Why would the crowd become angry at Jesus at these comments?

vs 28-30 How serious was the anger of the people in Nazareth towards Jesus?

Nazareth was a conservative Jewish town in 'Galilee of the Gentiles'. Bailey[12] points out that their Messianic hopes no doubt hinged around God judging the Gentiles and rewarding them with the spoils. The concept that Gentiles could receive God's blessing, especially over Jews, was abhorant to these Jews. But Jesus uses this opportunity to make it very clear that He was the Christ, the Messiah, for all peoples - the Kingdom of God is for all peoples. Being Jewish is now no longer the standard for receiving salvation, it is now by faith in the Messiah.

 Read Matthew 8:5-13

How does Jesus reinforce that the Kingdom of God is not automatic for Jews but is for all people based on faith in Christ?

---

12. Bailey 2008 p.152

Upside Down

Summary

Jubilee is a restoration to God's intended order, a liberation from the social structures based on greed and personal advancement. By invoking the Jubilee and his specific use of Isaiah 61 and specific reference to non-Jews, Jesus turns the Jewish leader's concepts of the kingdom upside down. His ministry as Messiah is one of proclamation of God's way, advocating justice for those who are oppressed, based on love and compassion, not law.

REFLECTION

It is unclear if the Hebrews still practiced Jubilee by the time of Jesus but it is unlikely.

What can you do in your life and ministry to practice Jubilee values?

What difference would it make in your community if land value was based on use until the 50th year?

Justice advocacy means speaking up for those who are oppressed or imprisoned in any way. What people are there in your community who need advocacy?

How much of your life and ministry is based on law or love and compassion for others, even if they are from another language or culture?

Turning the World

Notes

STUDY 6

THE CHARACTER OF THE KINGDOM
Matthew 5

Demonstrating the Kingdom

📖 Matthew 4:23-25 As Jesus went through Galilee, He demonstrated as well as talked about the Kingdom of God. List all the actions He took and the kinds of people He helped in these verses in Matthew 4:23-25:

If you were in Galilee at that time and saw Jesus doing these things, what kind of kingdom do you think He was talking about?

Why did large crowds follow him? What was their motive? Do you think they recognised Him as Messiah and King?

Turning the World

Matthew now introduces us to the teaching that Jesus gave to the crowds and to His disciples. The Kingdom of God has been called the Upside-down Kingdom because it turns the values of the world upside-down. Jesus now teaches about these values, starting with how the values of God's Kingdom are opposite to the values which society and religious life accepts as normal. We have already seen how Jesus refused Satan's temptations to come under the normal values of society.

Write down up to 8 character qualities that you or your church believe a successful Christian should have.

1.

2.

3.

4.

5.

6.

7.

8.

Upside Down

The Beatitudes

 Matthew 5:1-12

vs 3-10 How does Jesus frame the first and last verses in this poem to make sure people understood what His message was about?

List the 8 character traits that Jesus talks about, and how they are treated (the rewards) in the Kingdom of Heaven:

1.

2.

3.

4.

5.

6.

7.

8.

Would you say these are the kinds of character traits that we normally associate with being a successful Christian or spiritual leader? How do they compare with your list on the previous page?

Turning the World

Vs 11-12

Jesus actually goes further in these verses. What does He say about those who endure persecution because of Him?

Turning the law upside-down

 Matthew 5:13-48

Jesus now takes 8 topics where the Jewish ideas and laws were clear, and reinterprets them. List the topics and write how Jesus reinterprets them:

vs	Issue	Jesus' new interpretation
13-16	Salt &	Kingdom people are salt to flavour the world, stay salty..
	Light	Kingdom people are to be a light to the world, showing good works and leading people to praise God.
17-20		
21-26		

Upside Down

27-30

31-32

33-37

38-42

43-48

Turning the World

Summary

Jesus defines the character of God's Kingdom people while reinterpreting a number of key practical issues based on kingdom values.

REFLECTION

In Matthew 5:17-20 Jesus makes several statements about who will be called least, who will be called great, and who will not enter the Kingdom of Heaven. He affirms the Jewish law with a statement that He came to fulfil it, not abolish it. At the same time He criticises the empty "righteousness" of the teachers of the law and church leaders.

From what you have learned so far in this study, how has Jesus fulfilled the law?

What must our righteousness be based on to surpass that of the Pharisees?

Which of the character values discussed challenge you the most?

Upside Down

Notes

Turning the World

STUDY 7

KINGDOM BEHAVIOUR
Matthew 6

Matthew now turns his attention to Jesus' teaching about personal attitudes which govern behaviour – the behaviour of "Kingdom" people. His teaching the disciples how to pray is one of the most well known passages of the Bible, with "the Lord's Prayer" prayed by millions of people around the world on a daily basis. He also talks about treasures and rewards.

Giving to the poor

 Matthew 6:1-4

Jesus criticises the church leaders because they made sure everyone knew when they were giving to the needy. Who were they honouring?

How does Jesus say we should give to the needy?

What behaviour is rewarded by God in heaven?

The Lord's Prayer

 Matthew 6:9-15

Vs 5 What reward have the hypocrites (the church leaders) received by the way they pray?

Upside Down

Vs 6-8 What prayer behaviour does God reward?

Vs 9 Who should we address our prayer to, and where is He?

Vs 10 Where does God the Father reign as King at the moment?

Where should we pray for God's reign and will to go?

What will this look like - if the Kingdom of God was active in your life and that of your community? What would change?

Vs 11 How can we express our dependence on God?

Vs 12 Just as our feet get dirty from walking around and we wash them each day, how do we keep our spiritual lives clean each day?

Vs 14-15 If we want to be forgiven by God, what must be our attitude to those who have sinned against us?

The word for 'sins' or 'debts' here actually primarily refers to financial debts. How does this change your understanding of the Lord's prayer especially in the light of Jubilee practices?

Fasting

📖 Matthew 6:16-18

What fasting behaviour does God reward?

Possessions and money

📖 Matthew 6: 19-24

Vs 21 Where does Jesus say our heart is?

Vs 24 Why does Jesus say we cannot serve both these masters?

What will be our attitude towards God if we love money?

Food, drink and clothing, life's worries

📖 Matthew 6:25-34 What pictures does Jesus use as an example of how God takes care of us?

Vs 32 Does God know that we need these things? (also Vs 8, When does God know what our needs are?)

Upside Down

What type of people does Jesus say chase after them?

Vs 33 What should be our primary attitude to these things? Where should our focus be?

List all the times in Matthew 6 that Jesus talks about God the Father seeing and rewarding and why:

Turning the World

📖 Read Matthew 18:15-17.

Jesus expanded on this theme of forgiving others and states three steps to take if someone sins against you. What are they:

1.

2.

3.

📖 Matthew 18:18 & John 20:23.

What do you think Jesus means by saying that some things can be bound or loosed on earth and the same will happen in heaven? Do you think this relates to whether we forgive someone or not?

Summary

Jesus teaches on a number of issues related to finances, possessions and God's provision, challenging our heart attitude and desire to seek His kingdom first.

Upside Down

REFLECTION

How often does unforgiveness come because of financial matters, such as someone not repaying a loan?

Can this be an issue among church members?

Where would you honestly say your heart is focused?

What would it mean for you to "seek God's kingdom first"? What would need to change?

What needs do you have that you can ask God to meet?

Notes

STUDY 8

JESUS & THE RELIGIOUS LEADERS

Jesus upheld the Jewish religious system based on the Torah, the five Old Testament books of Genesis, Exodus, Leviticus, Numbers and Deuteronomy, and the other Old Testament writings. These formed the written law. But He was critical of the religious leaders of the day. Two main religious political parties dominated, the Pharisees and the Saducees.

The Pharisees were religioius legalists who lived by their complex "oral laws" which had been developed to expand on the written laws, and were handed down by oral tradition. While these were an attempt to ensure every contingency in daily life was covered by rules, they became overbearing for people. The Pharisees had become judgemental of those who did not follow these laws while they prided themselves in public display of piety.

The Saducees on the other hand were more liberal and maintained the written laws as paramount but developed business interests and landholdings, also fostering their relationship with the Romans while embracing the Greek (Hellenistic) culture of the day. They also did not believe in a resurrection.

Jesus confronts these religious leaders over four main issues.

Sabbath Day Observance

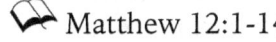 Matthew 12:1-14

vs 1-2 What was the first 'unlawful' event that disturbed the Pharisees?

Turning the World

vs 9-10, 13 What was the second 'unlawful' event?

vs 10, 14 What were the Pharisees trying to do?

vs 3-5, 11-12 What was Jesus' justification for breaking the law?

vs 7 What does Jesus say that God desires?

vs 12 The oral laws permitted someone to rescue a sheep, so how does Jesus respond to the supposed unlawfulness of healing someone on the Sabbath?

vs 6-8 The temple was considered to be the most holy and sacred place for the Jews, the centre of their religion. Jews would die defending it if needed. What are the astounding claims that Jesus makes here about Himself?

Jesus criticised the church leaders because they had allowed zeal for their oral laws, or traditions, to override their concern for people, which is at the heart of the written law of God. In doing so they had lost the heart of the Kingdom, which is based on values such as compassion and mercy.

Upside Down

Clean and Unclean

 Matthew 15:1-20

The OT law divided things into categories of clean or unclean (for example, Deuteronomy 14) and defined what would make people unclean. Rules for identifying religious contamination were many as was the need for cleansing acts to decontaminate people and make them religiously clean.

vs 1-2 What is the issue that the Pharisees target?

Where does this religious requirement come from?

vs 10, 16-20 What does Jesus say makes a person unclean?

vs 12 How did the Pharisees react to Jesus' statement?

vs 6-9 What does Jesus identify as the main problem with the Pharisees?

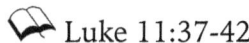 Luke 11:37-42

How does Jesus reply to this accusation that he did not wash before eating?

vs 41 What does Jesus say makes us clean?

Turning the World

vs 42 In criticising their extreme obsession with tithing, what kingdom values does he say they neglected?

vs 46 How does Jesus describe the result of all these laws on the people?

Jesus goes as far as saying that the church leaders actually negate or anull the Word of God, the written law, by their obsession with their oral traditions, the laws they had added.

Breaking Rules of Piety

📖 Matthew 9:9-13 Gentiles (non-Jews) were considered as unclean and Jews were prohibited from eating with them.

vs 11 What is the accusation of the Pharisees?

vs 12-13 What is Jesus' response?

Kraybill[13] notes:

> ... in Palestinian culture inviting a man to a meal is a sign of honour. It signals peace, trust, brotherhood, and forgiveness; sharing a table means sharing life. In Hebrew culture table-fellowship symbolised fellowship before God.... Jesus wining and dining with the religiously unclean is not merely a sign of His compassionate care but also represents their inclusion around the heavenly banquet table - their welcome into the community of salvation.

---

13. Kraybill 1978 p.174

Upside Down

Cleansing the temple

 Matthew 21:12-13

What did Jesus do to those who were buying and selling in the temple?

 Mark 11:15-18 How did the religious leaders respond?

 Matthew 21:12-13   What did Jesus accuse the people of doing?

The court of the Gentiles was set up in the outer courts of the temple and provided a place where even Gentiles could enter the temple precincts and pray. However the area had been turned into a lucrative market place. The Jerusalem temple was operated by the Saducees who gained immense wealth from the income. Money-changers converted ordinary money into temple money, and bird and animal sacrifices were sold in the market.

Jesus' attack was aimed at the Saducees, and targeted not only their profit-making business interests at the expense of worshippers (mainly the poor), but also the whole purpose of the temple, which the market place was desecrating by denying the Gentiles access to God. By disrupting the market, Jesus opened it up again to Gentiles, signalling once again that the new Kingdom of God was for Jew and Gentile.

In another sense, Jesus, who has proclaimed Himself as Lord of the Sabbath and Lord of oral tradition, now shuts the temple down (stopping the sale of sacrifices) emphasising that He is now Lord of the temple. Sacrifices will no longer be needed - His sacrifice will be the last.

Turning the World

📖 Matthew 12:6 How does Jesus describe His relationship to the temple?

📖 Matthew 5:17-20 Does Jesus regard the Pharisees and teachers of the law as members of the kingdom of heaven?

Summary

Jesus' criticism of the Pharisees, Saducees and religious leaders of the day highlighted the extent to which they had turned the intention of God through the laws on their head. The Kingdom of God turns them upside down again.

Piety is a matter of the heart, not outward display.

Mercy, justice and faith, not judgement over trivial traditions.

Worship and temple are for all people, not just Jews.

Religious and economic oppression have no place among God's people.

Jesus Himself is Lord of religion, the Kingdom of God returns to the foundation of God's intentions.

The Kingdom of God is different to Jewish religion.

REFLECTION

What traditions do you have in your church?

Are there unwritten ones that also have significant influence?

To what extent are they cultural traditions rather than Biblical traditions?

Do they reflect the Kingdom of God or are they confusing or even negating Kingdom values?

Notes

STUDY 9

THE FULFILLMENT OF THE KINGDOM
Matthew 24

Matthew tells us that Jesus preached that "the kingdom of heaven is near" as His central theme. What did Jesus mean and when does the Kingdom of God become 'here' rather than "near"?

 Matthew 10:7-8

When Jesus sent out the twelve disciples for ministry, what did He instruct them to preach?

What would be their ministry to validate the nearness of the Kingdom of God?

 Matthew 11:11-15

What does Jesus say about John the Baptist?

How does John compare to those who are "least in the kingdom"?

Turning the World

What are the two different time spans indicated by Jesus?

vs 12

vs 13

Why does Jesus call John "the Elijah who was to come"? (ref Malachi 4:5).

vs 12 What does Jesus say about the kingdom of heaven?

While Jesus praises John as being the greatest of the prophets of the Old Testament regime, He indicates that the kingdom of heaven has entered a new phase of growth since John. The coming of Jesus as Messiah introduced a new element of the nearness of the kingdom. The future King is now incarnate, living among us.

By definition, a kingdom is where people are the subjects of and loyal to a King.

 Matthew 12:28

What spiritual argument does Jesus use to claim the kingdom has come?

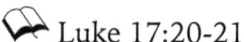 Luke 17:20-21

Where does Jesus say the kingdom is?

Jesus uses the title 'Father' often when speaking of God. For example in the Lord's Prayer.

Upside Down

Entering the Kingdom of God

 Matthew 10:40

What happens when we receive Christ?

 Matthew 10:32

What happens when we acknowledge Christ?

What happens when we disown Christ?

 Matthew 8:5-13

vs 8-10 When the Roman centurion (an officer in charge of 100 men) said he was a man who was under, or who understood, authority, why did Jesus praise him for his faith? Whose authority did he understand?

 Matthew 21:23-27

What did the chief priests and elders question Jesus about?

What does this tell you about their faith?

What is the relationship between faith and understanding authority?

Turning the World

📖 Matthew 28:18

What authority does Jesus claim after His resurrection?

📖 Matthew 8:11-12 Who is Jesus referring to as "many" (in vs 11), and the "subjects of the kingdom" (vs 12) who will be thrown out of the kingdom banquet?

📖 John 1:11-12

vs 11 Who are "his own" people that John speaks of? Why does he say they did not receive him?

vs 12 What do people have to do to become children of God?

📖 Acts 2:21, 38

vs 21 What does Joel say we need to do to be saved (ie. to enter the Kingdom of God)?

vs 38 What did Peter say we need to do to be saved?

Upside Down

 Matthew 7:21-23

What does Jesus say is the key to entering the kingdom of heaven?

Why would Jesus deny someone who had done miracles and cast out demons?

 Matthew 21:28-32

What did the tax collectors and prostitutes do to enter the kingdom ahead of the others (the religious Jews)? What did the others not do?

The Return of the King

There are a number of places where Jesus made it clear that there was a future fulfillment of the kingdom. There was a clear delimination between 'the present age' and the 'coming age'. "According to Matthew, the kingdom of heaven or the Messianic reign of Christ established on earth is to grow and extend itself until it reaches consummation".[1]

Ramsdell points out that while the Jews identified the coming age as commencing when the Messiah came, Jesus calls the 'coming age' as commencing with His second coming, so He has planted His kingdom on earth in the 'present age'.

---

1. Ramsdell 1984 p.131

Turning the World

📖 Daniel 7:9-18

vs 13-14 What authority is the person in his vision given? Who is this person?

vs 18 What will the saints receive?

📖 Matthew 24:30-31

How will Jesus return?

📖 Matthew 24:14

What will happen before this?

📖 Matthew 24:36

When does Jesus say this will happen?

While Jesus does not divulge a time and date, in Matthew 24 He nevertheless makes it clear that there are certain things historically and socially that will occur which give observers an indication that the time is near.

vs 27, 30 Do you think people all around the earth will know when Jesus returns?

Upside Down

📖 Ephesians 1:20-23

Where is Jesus now following His resurrection?

vs 21 Paul talks of the 'present age' and the 'age to come'. What status does Jesus have in both these periods?

The Consummation of the Kingdom of God

In the book of Revelation, John has a vision of the events leading up to the consummation or completion of the Kingdom of God. It is dominated by battles with Satan and his forces to gain control over the kingdom and concludes with their final defeat. What does this eschatological (or end times) kingdom look like? This is our best picture of heaven.

📖 Revelation 21-22 are our key Scriptures.

It should not surprise us, given the Jewish background of the story of salvation in Christ, that John's vision of the kingdom of heaven mirrors that of the prophetic writers of the Old Testament. Jerusalem as the city of David and heart of the nation of Israel is restored as place of peace. The temple as the focus of worship and sacrifice is also changed.

📖 Revelation 21:1-2 & 22:1-10 What does John say the new city is?

📖 Revelation 21:3-4 While Jerusalem is a city of buildings, and so descriptions of it such as in vs 11-21 focus on its physical splendor as a way of describing its magnificence in human terms, what does John now move the focus of the new Jerusalem to?

Turning the World

21 vs 21-22 Why did John not see a temple?

22 vs 3 Whose throne is in the city?

Read these OT prophesies and note what elements John applies to the final kingdom of heaven:

📖 Isaiah 65:17-25

📖 Isaiah 60:1-22

📖 Isaiah 25:8

📖 Isaiah 35:8-10

📖 Isaiah 11:1-10

📖 Revelation 21:24-26

Which people walk in the light of God's glory?

Is this a city for only Israelites?

Upside Down

21:12-14 Why do you think the vision of the Holy City has 12 foundations with the names of the apostles, and 12 gates with the names of the tribes of Israel on them?

Why do you think the city had gates on the North, South, East and West sides?

vs 25 When are the gates closed?

vs 27 What people can enter it?

📖 Revelation 7:9-10

What group of people does John see worshipping the Lamb?

📖 Revelation 21:8 Which people are excluded?

📖 Revelation 9:20-21 Why are they excluded?

77

Turning the World

Look up the Bible verses listed around the circle and write the key aspect that relates to what the fulfilled Kingdom of God will be like inside the circle[2]:

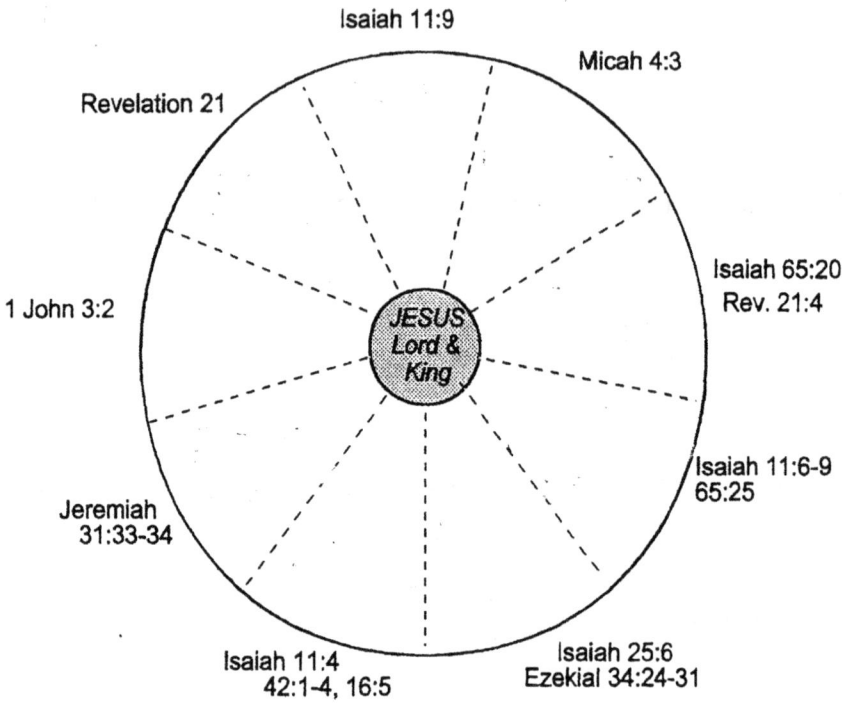

Summary

The Kingdom of God is consummated at the return of Jesus. Revelation gives an indication of the battles in the heavenly realm leading up to the final destruction of Satan and death.

With the coming of Jesus Christ to earth, and the establishment of the new covenant of grace through His death on the cross, people from all nations can enter into the kingdom through faith in Christ. However while living as humans, Christians live in the kingdom, "there but not yet". While God through His Spirit lives

2. From "God's Kingdom: mandate for mission, agenda for development, vision for the church" by Kirsten R Jack, 1997. Independent paper produced for Servants to Asia's Urban Poor mission.

in us and manifests God's kingdom in our hearts, we still live in a world dominated by Satan.

Until through resurrection we are transformed into new spiritual people and enter fully into the kingdom of heaven, the challenge for us is to live as subjects of the King, embodying the values of the Kingdom of God (in compassion and advocating justice), while witnessing to the risen Christ (proclamation).

Reflection

On the next page (for Notes) make a list of the things Jesus notes in Matthew 24 that will come or happen before His appearance.

What new things about the fulfillment or consummation of the Kingdom of God have you learnt today?

How has your view of heaven changed through this study?

How does knowing that the Kingdom of God in its fullness will become a reality in the future help you live day to day?

Turning the World

Notes

STUDY 10

KINGDOM AND JUDGEMENT
The Parables in Matthew

The theme of judgement is a major one throughout Scriptures. In the Old Testament, judgement of Israel's enemies and of Israel itself for not wholeheartedly following God's laws was a common message particularly by the prophets.

In the New Testament judgement focuses more at a personal level, with people judged for their individual stand against God demonstrated in their actions. However Jesus still has a message of judgement for the Pharisees, Saducees and religious leaders.

Jesus prefaced most of his parables by saying, "The kingdom of heaven is like ..." Nearly all parables have a warning of judgement.

The Parable of the Tenants

 Matthew 21:33-46

vs 40-41 What do the chief priests and elders reply to Jesus' question?

Who is the landowner in the story?

Who are the servants that are treated badly?

Who is the son who was killed?

Turning the World

vs 43 What warning does Jesus give the Jewish religious leaders?

Who are the other people who will receive the kingdom?

vs 45 Did they understand His meaning? How did they respond?

This is one of the most direct statements by Jesus that Gentiles will gain the kingdom and that some Jews may even be excluded.

The Parable of the Weeds

Matthew 13:24-30

Why did the owner not want his servants to pull up the weeds?

When will the separation of weeds and wheat happen?

What happens to the weeds?

Matthew 13:36-43 - Jesus explains the parable.
What is the field and what does the good seed stand for?

Upside Down

Who are the weeds and who sows them?

When is the harvest and who does the harvesting?

 Revelation 14:14-20

In this fulfillment of the parable, in John's vision there are two harvests. The second harvest is specifically for which people, and what is the result?

The Parable of the Net

 Matthew 13:47-50

In this parable, which two groups are separated, and what is their end?

 Galatians 3:6; 2 Corinthians 5:21; Galatians 2:20-21

How do we become righteous in God's sight?

Do we need to fear this judgement time at the end of the age if we are in Christ?

Turning the World

The Final Judgement

 Revelation 20:11-15

vs 12 What are people judged on and where is this recorded?

vs 15 What happens if your name is not recorded in this book?

 Daniel 7:9-10

Who is the judge and how many people were being judged in this court?

7:18 Who will receive the kingdom and how long will they possess it for?

 1 Corinthians 1:2

Sanctified and holy come from the same Greek root from which the word 'saint' is derived. According to this greeting by Paul, who are the saints?

 Philippians 4:3

What does Paul say about the people he mentions, his fellow workers in the cause of the gospel?

So if those in Christ, the saints, whose names are in the book of life, are not judged in this court, is there another judgement?

The Parable of the Talents

 Matthew 25:14-30

vs 24 Why was the servant with one talent afraid and what did he do?

What is the point of this parable do you think?

The Parable of the Sheep and Goats

 Matthew 25:31-46

vs 32 What people are referred to here, and what are the two categories separated?

There is no doubt that this parable is referring to the end times judgement.

vs 35-36 What is the criteria that the King uses to judge people?

vs 37-39 What do the "righteous" sheep reply?

vs 40 What is the bottom line action they did?

Turning the World

vs 45 What action did the "wicked" goats not do?

There is sometimes confusion over this story, and that it says we are saved because of our actions of mercy. However, the King makes it clear that the righteous sheep demonstrated their faith through their selfless actions of mercy. In their kingdom lifestyle of compassion, they served others and by doing so served Christ. The goats didn't even think about others and were judged accordingly. As Jesus said, 'where your heart is, there is your treasure'.

 James 2:14-26

What does James say about the relationship between faith and action?

vs 17 What does he say is a dead faith?

Parable of the Unmerciful Servant

 Matthew 18:21-35

vs 27 How did the king respond to the servant's plea for mercy?

vs 28 How did the servant respond to his fellow servant who owed money?

vs 35 What does God expect from people in the Kingdom of God?

Upside Down

The Parable of the Ten Unmarried Women

Matthew 25:1-13

Why did five of the women get locked out of the wedding feast?

What did the wise ones do?

Jesus told this parable immediately after his teaching on His return in Matthew 24. What do you think is the main point of the parable? Is it about salvation or is it about what we do as kingdom people?

There are many encouragements in the New Testament to make sure that we live to honour God.

1 Corinthians 10:31 When should we glorify God in our actions?

Romans 12:9-21

Paul gives a list of actions that reflect kingdom values. Read through this list and note any that you need to improve on in your life.

Turning the World

Summary

A true Christian should not fear judgement because their name is recorded in the book of life through faith in Christ for salvation. But those whose names are in the book of life should be living out the values of the Kingdom of God, and demonstrating those values through their proclamation, justice advocacy and compassion.

REFLECTION

Which of the parables of Jesus speaks most clearly to you about the kingdom of heaven?

Would you consider your faith 'dead' according to James' definition of faith?

How do the parables challenge you to make some changes in your life and ministry?

Jesus seems to make a distinction between those who are doing miracles in His name and claim to be of the kingdom of heaven but are not, and those who are not practicing good deeds. What is the difference?

Notes

STUDY 11

KINGDOM AND CHURCH

The question now remains - is the church the Kingdom of God?

We have already seen that there are three time periods evident in the New Testament teachings:

1. The period of the Old Covenant of law, equating to the Old Testament period, with John the Baptist being the last prophet.

2. The "present age", which commenced with the coming of Jesus Christ and his ministry and the introduction of the New Covenant of grace.

3. The "age to come", the fulfilled Kingdom of God, which is ushered in when Jesus returns.

Which period is the 'era of the church' that we are we in today?

To understand the Kingdom of God in the "present age", we need to consider some Messianic prophesies in more detail.

 Isaiah 49

vs 3 What does God call Israel?

 Genesis 12:1-3

Who did God want to bless through Abraham and the nation that would come from his descendants?

 Isaiah 49:4 What emotion does God express about Israel now through the prophet?

Upside Down

Israel did not meet the hopes God had for it to be a blessing and bring salvation to all nations, Gentiles as well as Jews. This culminated in the Jewish leaders killing Jesus and rejecting Him as the Messiah appointed by God.

Just as we have seen that the city of Jerusalem in Biblical prophesy has a second spiritual meaning, so the 'servant' passages have a second meaning.

 Isaiah 49:5-9 Who would you identify as the servant?

vs 6 What will he do?

vs 7-13 How many things can you identify in these verses that relate directly to Jesus or stories about him? How many reflect Jubilee?

 Zechariah 3:8-9

What will the servant, the Branch, do?

Turning the World

📖 Isaiah 11

Who was Jesse (ref. Matthew 1:6)? Who is the Branch?

📖 Isaiah 42:1-4

What will the servant bring and who will he bring it to?

The role of the Messiah was like two sides of a coin, one side servant, the other King. Jewish perceptions of the Messiah at the time of Jesus were of a miltary ruler who would overthrow the Roman oppressors and bring freedom to Israel. This blinded their eyes to see Jesus come first as the Servant.

📖 Isaiah 9:1-7

How do these verses clearly identfy the coming King as Jesus?

What verse indicates miltary victory over oppressors?

📖 Isaiah 32:1

How will the King reign?

📖 Zechariah 9:9-12

What Jubilee values does Zechariah claim for the king?

Upside Down

What parts of this prophesy are fulfilled by Jesus?

 Philippians 2:5-11

What Messianic role did Jesus take on earth?

What role did God give Him after His ascension?

Somehow the Jewish leaders, in their focus on expectations of military liberation, failed to recognise Jesus as the Servant. However Jesus will return as the liberating King when He comes again, thus fulfilling both aspects of Messianic prophesy.

We know that Jesus' constant message was that 'the kingdom of heaven is near'.

 Luke 17:21

Where does Jesus say the kingdom is? Can you see God's Kingdom by looking for it somewhere?

 John 18:33-37

In response to Pilate's questions, Jesus affirms His Kingship. Where does He say his kingdom is?

Turning the World

We know that after Jesus returns, the Kingdom of God in "the age to come" will be fully established as a place where the saints are gathered with Christ. It will though be different to earthly places because it will be spiritual in nature and people will have resurrected bodies, another dimension beyond the physical.

So how do we describe the church? If it is not the kingdom of heaven yet, what is it? The kingdom is within us but has no structure we can describe. It is in our hearts but belongs somewhere else. So we can perhaps best describe it this way:

The church is the people who have entered into the Kingdom of God by faith in Christ and declare Him as King.

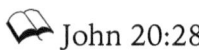 John 20:28

How does Thomas's statement reflect this definition?

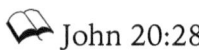 Romans 10:9

How does this teaching from Paul combine the two elements?

Kraybill[3] suggests:

> Today God rules through the presence of His Holy Spirit.... The church is the body of Christ composed of individuals living in obedient discipleship to the way of Jesus.

When we talk about church today, we are usually referring to a building or a group activity such as worship or preaching.

> Today we must distinguish between the kingdom and the institutionalised church. The kingdom that Jesus announced points us to something greater than ourselves and our own

---
3. Kraybill 1978 p.188ff

structures. The New Testament does not make the kingdom synonymous with the church.[4]

To accomplish its goals, the body of Christ needs social, administrative and political structures, "social vehicles or servant structures.... to meet their own needs and to serve others".[5] They are not the church but are likened to the skins of the church, the visible efforts of God's people when they gather for worship, prayer, fellowship, Sunday School, teaching, outreach or mission.

Identify the 'servant structures' of the early church, the practical aspects of organising church and ministry, in these verses:

📖 Acts 2:42-47; 4:32-35 First church

📖 Acts 15:1-3 Antioch church

📖 Acts 15:4-6, 12 Jerusalem church conference

📖 Acts 13:1-3 Antioch church mission

---

4. Kraybill 1978 p.187
5. Kraybill 1978 p.189

Turning the World

📖 Acts 18:28 Apollos' ministry

📖 Acts 19:9 Paul's teaching ministry

While 'servant skins', the institutional or practical structures of the local Body of Christ, are determined by the expression of God's Kingdom desired and the leading of God's Spirit, they will reflect cultural values in the local context. This can include things like language and cultural ways of communicating and culturally appropriate ways of personal conduct, etiquette and dress.

The values behind these skins must always reflect the values of the Kingdom of God as expressed in the Word of God, which enables change within cultures to occur as God's' people align more with the values of the kingdom.

This means that the expression of the Kingdom of God will vary in time to meet changes in culture. A ministry to the poor will look different in a western big city than in a rural village in a developing nation. However the ministries of proclamation and values of justice, compassion, love and mercy that express the Kingdom of God must be maintained in each context.

The Jewish religious leaders were very keen on maintaining the status quo of their traditions and observances, but they had drifted a long way from the values of the kingdom. The church too can be in danger of holding onto inappropriate structures when they are no longer expressing the values of God's Kingdom.

We can expand on and summarise the focus of kingdom ministries by creating an 'Agenda for kingdom mission' in the diagram next page.

Upside Down

The Agenda of the Kingdom

In the circle on page 78 we noted some key aspects of the fulfilled Kingdom of God. These aspects now lead us to consider what God's agenda for the church on earth is, an agenda which reflects the fulfilled Kingdom.

Read the Bible verses listed around the circle below[6] and write in the key activity mentioned in the circle sections - these should be the activities which are going to lead to the advancement of the Kingdom of God on earth. These are the activities of the true servants of the King and give us a mission agenda for the church.

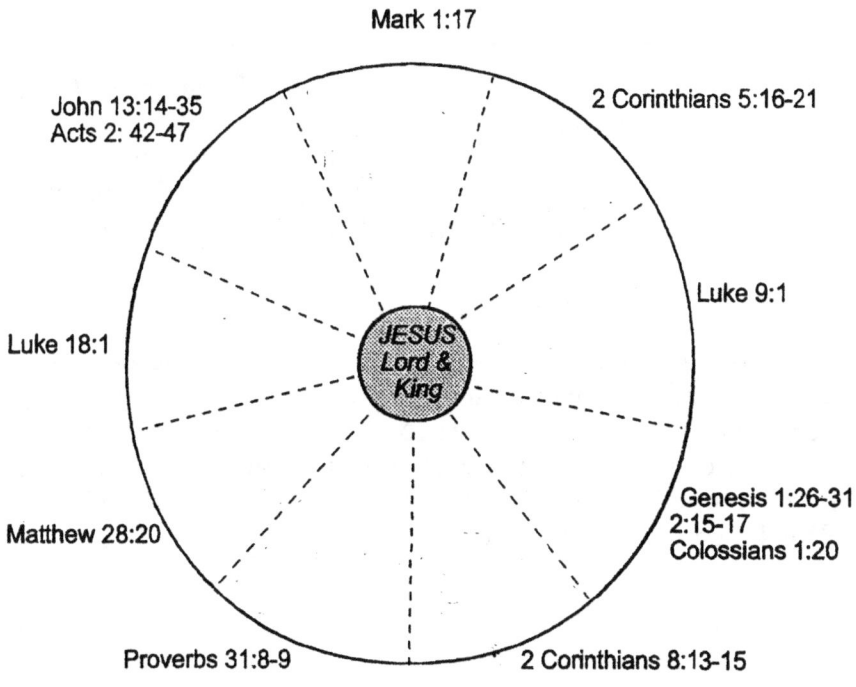

Identify stories from the life and ministry of Jesus that are examples of the ministry aspects you have noted in the circle.

---

6. From Kirsten R Jack, 1997.

Turning the World

How do these aspects reflect the values of Jubilee and Jesus' ministry mandate in Luke 4 (from Isaiah 61)?

Summary

While neither Israel nor the church are the Kingdom of God, where people have come under the Lordship of Jesus, the kingdom exists in them. The corporate gathering of these people is an expression of the kingdom, visible through servant structures they create to be able to meet their social, religious and mission activities.

The continual challenge to the Body of Christ is to ensure that the values of God's Kingdom are not reduced even if its structures become obsolete, controlled by people or out of date with society. There is a constant need to review the 'servant' structures of the church in the light of their cultural context to ensure the witness of the kingdom within that context is not lost.

Upside Down

Reflection

How would you define the church?

What 'servant skins' do you have in your own church or denomination?

Are there any structures or traditions that are observed in your church which are no longer expressing Kingdom of God values? What can you do to restore or release them?

Are there any situations in your community or cultural context that need a structural response to demonstrate or express the agenda of the Kingdom of God?

What values are you living day to day which are not contributing to the welfare and witness of the Body of Christ in your location?

What will you do to change them?

NOTES

Bibliography

Bailey, Kenneth E., *Jesus Through Middle Eastern Eyes* by Kenneth E. Bailey. Copyright (c) 2008 by Kenneth E. Bailey. Used by permission of Intervarsity Press, PO Box 1400, Downers Grove, IL 60515, USA.

Jack, Kristen R., *God's Kingdom: mandate for mission, agenda for development, vision for the church*, 1997. Independent paper produced for Servants to Asia's Urban Poor mission.

Kraybill, Donald B., *The Upside-Down Kingdom*, Scottdale PA: Herald Press, 1978.

Ramsdell, Thomas J., *The Kingdom of Heaven in the Gospel of Matthew*, The Biblical World, vol. 4, no. 2, 1894, pp. 124–133. JSTOR, www.jstor.org/stable/3135427.

Wuest, Kenneth S., *The New Testament, An Expanded Translation* by Kenneth S. Wuest, Riverside Book and Bible House, 1984.

www.ingramcontent.com/pod-product-compliance
Lightning Source LLC
Chambersburg PA
CBHW051954290426
44110CB00015B/2243